It Is. What It Is...
and ... It's Gone Be.
What It's Gone Be.

Tristian Bellegarde

It Is. What It Is... and ... It's Gone Be. What It's Gone Be. © 2023 Tristian Bellegarde

All rights reserved.

No part of this publication may be reproduced, stored in a retrieval system, or transmitted, in any form or by any means, electronic, mechanical, photocopying, recording or otherwise, without the prior written permission of the presenters.

Tristian Bellegarde asserts the moral right to be identified as author of this work.

Presentation by *BookLeaf Publishing*

Web: www.bookleafpub.com

E-mail: info@bookleafpub.com

ISBN: 9789357212960

First edition 2023

*BIGGEST AND MOST LOVING appreciation
to my mom. Theresa, you never gave up on me
THANK YOU FOR EVERYTHING YOU
TAUGHT AND CONTINUE TO BLESS ME
WITH!*

ACKNOWLEDGEMENT

Cindy Grey and Uncle Dion

PREFACE

I am just happy to be sharing my truths with all and every.

Hello

The first day which is, Monday November 21, 2022! Honestly all I wanted to do was say HELLO! As this is the most common approach to me and what you are going to experience! I'm really excited and nervous to embark on this journey with myself firstly, with integration of the audiences to come! As I began today's inspiration, I thought about the experiences I've been having. BEAUTIFUL. I learnt of the basic concept behind the Japanese inspired saying/word. "Wabi Sabi" and "Maryabi". To me they represented, "No Worries" and "A Beginning" of something. I ended up finding the actual definitions soooo similar to my understanding of understanding. Check out the definitions for yourself and have yourself an innovating time if you so choose? These are the last words here although and Enjoy!

Once Upon A Time 11-22

2

Once upon a time I used to be so faithful
Once upon a time I used to be supportive and believe
Once upon a time I had a vision of what I thought perfection could be
Once upon a time in a FAAAAAAR away land
Sometimes I sit with myself, and we have.... we have the most brilliant of conversations
The one vision and version that has not seemed to switch up on myself is the SKY! So pretty and so blue looking like true freedom
I don't exactly know what's happened to make me dissolve my competence to assess my needs it seems
This is not the way that I envisioned my version of "Once Upon A Time"

Who I always wanted to be...

November 21st This date. I want to add the
numbers.
I am in my own. In a loving, and solidifying
capacity.
I feel so important in my own stature today.
I was thinking about who I am and who I've
become today.
I've surprised myself with who I've become.
I am so proud of myself and who I've become.
I've surprised myself in many ways as I'm sure I
have others.
To date. I don't think I have any secrets left.
Once upon a time I was so secretive.
For reasons I'll never be able to explain.
Today. I will and can say. I am.
I am.
I am me. I am happy. I am worthy.
I would never want to be anywhere else but
where I am now.
I love myself and I appreciate all those around
me.
All of those who believe in me.
THANK YOU! THANK YOU! THANK YOU!

Not... Just another day...

Yesterday was not a day like most
The reason for this was I was feeling quite
indisposed
There was a feeling of being discombobulated
Feeling like everything was in a haze, basically
wasted

This feeling really hurt my heart and soul
The realization that I have lost control
The power is no longer mine to keep
It really shook me deep

33 Balance

There are days that I always see repeating numbers. It's a commonality for me to see 11:11. Almost twice each day. Day after day. Lately I have been seeing the repetitive numbers: 3:33 or 33 and 66. I'm not quite sure what this means but I am sure there is a major significance to myself. Why me? I'm not exactly sure why or what to interpret here, but I think that I should start paying attention. One of the reasons why I may be feeling this way is because I am going to be 33 in my next year of existence. I am feeling rather positive in this aspect also! I have always been a person that seems to follow my feeling over everything else. This is a good and bad thing at times... As I entitled this entry it was expressing to me as in (3 and 3 or 3 of 3. Balance and equality. BALANCE AND EQUALITY. 3 goes into 3, into itself and become zero. I don't exactly know how to express this because I got 2 different feelings with this explanation. It could feel like perfection to some and to others it could make you feel like... The fact that this number becomes itself, makes it become nothing. Not nothing in a bad way but it seems nothing as

INFINITE. Never ending, maybe never even starting but still the fact remains it once had an existence.

Always Be Authentic: Showing Appreciation

Day1, this was the day that it all began. When I say day1, this comes with so many "connections, synchronicities or coincidences". All those big words with the same and most beautiful kind of meaning. Simple and pure like a few of my favorite sounds in life. A child's laughter or "innocence". As they grow and you watch them learn how to say their ABC's and 123's. When you can literally feel the love language of a Loon's call, greeting the world in the early morning. 3 numbers chosen from 0-1000 with angel # meanings:

 #778 - Finding the sense of Life

 #3 - Creativity and Optimism. Being open to the possibility of Life

 #9 - Combinations of culmination, Wisdom and experience

Other favorites I discovered in my search were holidays and smells. Canada Day goes awesome with Cotton Candy. Watermelons are green, just like the main color associated with St. Patty's Day. Lastly Easter, the holiday of eats and sweets. Mmmmm, Lemon Meringue Pie. The reason I started this particular piece of work was

because I wanted to learn about a few of my
people. Authenticity means -
Realistic/True/Legitimate. Make life worth
living. Create Happiness; and Be Happiness.

Confessing My Most Terrible Secret

It would take 5000 cries of "I hate you" to take away my pride.
4000 slaps to the face before I bowed down to you.
3000 people laughing at me because of you to make me cry.
2000 eagles swarming round in the sky to scare me.
1000 times of a broken heart to hurt me.
100 shouts of "NO!" to surprise me.
And 1 saying of "I don't love you anymore" to break me.

Random Thoughts... Thought by Yours Truly

<3 -Time is of the Essence. People always give into what you what you oppose, especially after you come to your senses. *Reverse Psychology*
<3 - The world is not always a kind place, so we need to learn to love ourselves as well as show ourselves compassion. It's the only thing stopping you from living fully!
<3 - It Is What It Is, and It's Gone Be What It's Gone Be... Don't trust anyone not even my damn self. The only one that's GOT ME IS ME! Buuut, then again to think about it. Even your Shadow leaves you on a cloudy day.

The First Half of the Year (in monthly description)

January-(Guardian Angels)- New Year, New Time, New Me, New You. Throw away the fear. See the sign. And then who could be you.
February-(Heartaches)- Beauty sparks in many ways at different times. What do you see when you see beauty? Is it in looks, personality or both? What is your most desired feature and what does it take to make or break you?
March-(Womans Pride)- You make things as you need them. See them as you want them. Do them as they come and believe them as they're done.
April-(Fulfillment)- Flowers bloom and memories stay. Becoming a new person in every way. Happy times and selfless dreams. Snow melts and then comes the Spring.
May-(Fam-ILY)- Love is what keeps my family life going. I love my family with everything I have, and NOTHING can ever change that! BOO-YAH!!!
June-(L.B.B.F.N Home)- There is so much to be proud of when you come from a First Nations background. BE proud of who you are and never put your head down. Keep your head held high!!!

The Second Half of the Year (in monthly description)

July-(Bellegarde)- Look into the eyes of us. Do you see what we see? Can you tell me who we are? Life and Love into one is what we make.! **August** Looking through my calendar, I seem to have left that one completely out!! I didn't notice til close to 13 years later... How odd.

September-(Alvin Francis Sr.)- Like the wind blows, the leaves change color. People die and others are born. It is the time to start over as the seasons change again. Let the secret hearts release their mourn.

October-(Promises Made)- Peek-a-boo!!! I C U! Scary times and fun rides. Up and down we go. Roller-coaster take me away now, thankful for the life I live. Every day is a blessing. Count them and see how many you find.

November-(Balance)- Sadness evails with the color of Black. Yellow, White and Red. No time for turning back. Keep this faith in the way that you proceed. Always remember that you are never truly alone.

December-(MnM)- This is a Beautiful time in my life. I have my new beginnings. I have everything I could ever want and need. NEW BEGINNINGS is what it is.

How Would You Feel

As she sat there and thought about all the
emotions and experiences, she was having in
that moment she thought to herself, "What am I
doing wrong?"
It kept running through her mind everything she
had done in the last 24 hours
She could not remember if it was something she
said or did
She prayed over and over again, hoping for a
simple sign
There were many of them being given but none
that were visible to her
She had exhausted every one of her resources
Every last bit of the strength she had,
unknowingly, put away
Trying to convince herself that it was worth
saving
The memories, pleasant and sweet, painful yet
pleasurable
Were the auras brought to physical dimensions
due to one emotion
One, four letter emotion
LOVE

My Sister Forever 31

It really astounds me how beautiful the world can present itself to be. Picture this, the beginning of Summer. A day in the middle of May, a little closer to becoming June. You're driving in a serene and still scenery. The trees are a luxurious and deep green, while the hills roll on for miles. Thinking about the breathtaking sights, I am blessed to see breaks my heart. One of my very first friends began her journey to her forever home last night. I'll be honest I worried for her at times, but never did I expect to live through this reality. I don't think its fully even hit me yet. I remember the days when we were barely teenagers always causing quiet ruckus. As we got older, we would grow to make memories I will never forget. A lot of them were quite simply, simple. Truly I don't even want to use that word. They were more like embracing. I say embracing because the moments we shared would we shared helped to shape my later life experiences. She was a unique being, with a gorgeous and authentic smile. It makes me miss my late sister, Tiffany even more today! Now they are up in the skylights popping off without me! That's has to be ok though because I ain't done down here and they completed what needed to be done, while leaving real impressions on all they people! You done good my sister! I love you and I pray you will watch over those of us that are still completing our tasks. As I am finishing up what I write the Sun wants to start shining. This confirms to me that even though I'm not saying it out-loud, I know you know what's up! H.R.J.N Fly High My Sister You're Finally Free! Say hi to Tiff for me and don't forget to save my seat beside ya'll because at the end we gotta be that cool.

Over and Over Again

The words that go through my mind as I read the title are exactly those... In lyric form although. For those of you that may not catch the reference I am referencing the song "Over and Over- Tim McGraw/Nelly. Such an amazing song many moons ago! They sing, "It's all in my head, keeps playing over and over again". A very heartfelt song, involving lost loves. The difference between then and now is that back then I was singing along with the words feeling pains of a heartache I surely had no experience of. Really putting true feeling into what I repeated along with them. Not really thinking about anything but the moment I was presently in. Those were more simple and less complicated times. I'm not exactly sure how less complicated they were or if the only complications I face now are of my own doing? I place a thought on the fact that I now pay more attention. Now that I think about this, I'm not so sure this is all about being 'Over and Over Again. For some odd reason it's feeling a bit more like Deja-vu.

Unknown- 2013

Sweet surrender is what I want to succumb to, if only in the arms of the most justified. I've been sitting here thinking about where I am and where I've been. It's just a constant contemplation, am I doing the right thing? I'm worried it's not. I just need to stop this journey I am on because I honestly feel like there is more to life than what I am doing now. I used to be someone before, now I feel like a nobody because I put my life on hold for someone else. Now I still want to be with that someone. My life also feels so lonesome like something is missing. I feel like I'm floating. I don't know where I put all my worth into. I know I should be myself but that's hard to do when you no longer know you are or where you want to be.

Regretful Memories

Have you ever felt regret? Honestly do you know what it's like to hurt someone, put them down and feel no regret at that time. Memories brought into my mind, ones that I think about day in and day out. This is what has intimidated me to write this. These memories, these regretful memories are mocking me and encouraging me, encouraging me to try make the same mistake twice. So I have been ever so carefully watching myself, taking my steps slowly, keeping an eye on what I thought was to be righteousness towards committing and fulfilling good deeds.

Happy Moments of A Fallen Angel

The needs that people feel for desire have been rather incapable of making happy moments. Sitting back, making the moment more worthwhile is the fun part. Coming from above you see the beautiful Angel, she has been a gift sent from God. Where is God, who is he? This beautiful figure has been sent with a message to help the ones in need. There are so many problems that go on in one's life, but never give up. Look to the Fallen Angel.

Beautiful- A birthday gift for my Mom Theresa Mary

The essence of your beauty, That has caught me,
If looks could only kill, The world would be still
Like the siren that sings, Here I am hypnotized,
Here I am to be blind, From the look of your
pretty brown eyes
The unconditional love, Only a mother could
love, Such a privilege I have, To be born from
such beauty
Beautiful more than anything, That is what they
say, It's so true no lying, On March 8th that day
There was a miracle given to the world, The day
that you came into this world, With all my heart,
I will love you forever
Because you are so beautiful, I have to feel
special, I envy nothing about you, I wish I were
you
Nothing would ever change, So perfect in every
way, I say it now every day, Mommy your so
beautiful

I Won't Forget

22

Lost in thought, oblivious to the world around
me.
Today I am forced to sit down and decide within
myself, what I want in life.
I'm also forced to give up a part of myself. Grow
up, realize...
No I already see emotional tragedy and drama.
A very strong passion unlived to reality.
Deep meaning felt, unbelievable loyalty to one
but not the other.
 Undying honesty finally revealed the true me.

Invisible Ghost

Invisible ghost in my mind who keeps floating
in and out of my life. Why do you make me love
you so?
Why is it that you love me with such a passion
you hold onto me even after death. Your there no
one can see you but me.
It pains me every time I live my life because you
are a part of me.
The part of me, the ghostly figure that makes me
go crazy.
You whisper in my ear. I hear what you say, but I
don't understand.
How can it be that you love only I after I let yo
go.
Rainy days express my determination. You've
corrupted me invisible ghost.
I love you, but at the same time it can't possibly
be real... can it?

Feelings. What is Real? Confused.

I can't do this anymore. I'm scared of what's to come, the consequence of my decision still to be made. So many possibilities of the circumstance on which upon I stand. The words I want to breathe are so sweet and should be savored for the moment that they are said. Feelings are all things that aren't even real in life. We make choices to determine the future that we look into everyday but really what is the future? Something we look into that doesn't exist? See here I am being confused what do I do. I want to be with you but do you want me? If something does happen can I count on you to be the only real thing in the world where I am surprised, confused, complicated and happy to have all at once, will this be my childhood fantasy fulfilled from my dreams of when I was a little girl. Where are we going to go, how do you think this will work, if anything will it be real? The words and sayings in my head express me and what I'm about but when you read them is it like your reading me do you understand what I say when I have the courage to express it all to the max of everything. I'll never know what this can or will

be if I don't try but what does try mean? Will I
ever know, are you going to teach me, will I
understand, please just give me a chance so we
could figure out what is real.

A Beginning. A Middle. An End.

As with every book or story that most of us have read there are always three parts, right? My "Introduction", (seems more fitting for description), started when I inserted the poem entitled HELLO! I was so excited to begin this journey and now it has run its course. Is it funny that I don't want to call this last one an "End"? I'm not too sure on that one, but I guess to each their own. So as this is my not ending but last part of this book, I just want to give a great big THANKS to ALL who have possibly decided to see what I wanted to share, as I reflected on these last 21 days. I brought together parts of myself that I am proud to be presenting to the world. I have an inkling this may not be a one-time gig for myself going forward. Then again, I seem to have new ideas everyday about how I want to be seen and remembered in this world. I have surprised myself with what I produced but I am also very proud of what I have created as well. Last message to all... Please remember to be kind to YOURSELF and OTHERS! Nothing but Love til next time.